Y0-ACG-469

LIGHT FALLS THROUGH YOU

LIGHT FALLS
THROUGH YOU

ANNE SIMPSON

M&S

National Library of Canada Cataloguing in Publication Data

Simpson, Anne, 1956–
Light falls through you

Poems.
ISBN 0-7710-8077-8

I. Title.

PS8587.I54533L53 2000   C811'.54   C00-930000-7
PR9199.3.S526L53 2000

We acknowledge the financial support of the Government of
Canada through the Book Publishing Industry Development
Program for our publishing activities. We further acknowledge the
support of the Canada Council for the Arts and the Ontario Arts
Council for our publishing program.

Typeset in Centaur by M&S, Toronto
Printed and bound in Canada

McClelland & Stewart Ltd.
The Canadian Publishers
481 University Avenue
Toronto, Ontario
M5G 2E9
www.mcclelland.com

2 3 4 5   04 03 02 01

Paul

Contents

SOUVENIRS

Descent	1
Deer on a Beach	2
Light Falls Through You	4
Grammar Exercise	6
Chopping Wood	7
In Italy	9
Salamander	10
Octopus	12
A Head Like Hers	13
Shoulder of Water, Skin of Air	14
Luna Moth	15
Sea of Death	17
Feeding the Anchoress	19
Myth	20
Meanwhile, in Ithaca	22
July 15, 1887	24
White, Mauve, Yellow	26
Flying East	28
Two Photographs	30
Archeology	31
Small	33

USUAL DEVICES

>	37
,	38
!	40
+	41
=	43
;	44
:	45
( )	48
?	49
•	52
RELIQUARY	55
ALTARPIECE	61
Notes	77
Acknowledgements	79

LIGHT FALLS THROUGH YOU

Souvenirs

DESCENT

The *Hector* brought emigrants to Nova Scotia in the eighteenth century.

Water isn't treacherous
nor is the descent into it,
made easy by a plank held
at an angle on the ship's rail
so that a small girl wrapped
in a length of flannel could drop
quickly. In the silence
after her body slid on the wood
and the brief splash
I recalled nothing of her,
not the undulating terrain
of her skin, not the sleeping
animal of her hand
in mine, not even the cleft in her chin
which I used to touch,
marvelling.

DEER ON A BEACH

Once in Africa I heard voices wailing, then turned a bend
in a muddy track and saw the wagon full of women,

faces greased with white, like a chorus from a Greek tragedy,
reminders – strophe and antistrophe – of what was lost.

Yesterday, when the beach was blindfolded with snow,
I found parts of a deer. My daughter wouldn't look

at the elegant hoof (which I lifted with the tip
of my boot) or the half-ellipse of jawbone. She hung back,

afraid, while I examined the hide, and the way it seemed
to be cut, slashed from the body. I could see the lining

of red, like an opera cloak. The head was gone, and the antlers,
but I didn't think about this until further up the beach,

where I saw the two forelegs, stuck in a drift
of snow feathered with animal hair. Grief has no words,

only a trailing off into things remembered
inaccurately. Months ago we'd seen a doe a half-mile away,

sleek and young, in the sparse woods above the beach, her flanks
heaving gently. We left the beach – where the ocean had thrust

glassy fragments of ice into the soft strip of land — and climbed
the steps to a little deck. Below us, the remnants of the deer,

cast here and there, did not keep us from looking further out
to where the frozen sea, in folds and dips and pans, spread white,

unmoving. But something had changed, as if a lock in the cold air
had clicked open with a key. The ice was cracking, abruptly;

we shuffled up the next slippery flight of steps,
and through the woods. We saw crisscrossed tracks

of deer and dog, and perhaps snowshoe hare, though human
prints obscured them in places. I thought of the deer's small, cloven

hoof, and its fur, threaded brown and gold. Trophies not taken. Nothing
was left but tidbits for the crows: such food, stinking of violence,

comes from our world, not the next. Death gets into it
one way or another, a voice that follows wherever we go.

After many years avoiding the place, I lift the latch
(which disappears as it is touched) and find

you are young as always, while I have closed thousands
of little doors in my skin. Perhaps small words, such as love,

still exist, floating through air in the far distance. Like kites,
they come back when I pull on them, so I've lost

nothing, not even your hands, full of something discarded:
the nests of birds, complete with eggs, or feathery ostrich ferns.

But look, there is snow on the floorboards, where the wind
brings it under the door. You are in shadow and then light,

as you lean forward. Now I see wrens hiding in your hair,
field mice scampering down your leg. I pause, catching the scent

of earth, and realize your arms are moss, fingers about to blossom –
the wrong season, but never mind, your eyes are the same,

uncannily. I see everything planted in you unfurling new leaves
and flourishing. I reach out fondly, at the same moment

sunlight falls through you. After all, I should have known
you would dissolve into something clear and unresolved,

like water, and that I would put my hands deep in you
and they would come up empty, wet from the touch of my own face.

GRAMMAR EXERCISE

In December 1992, students in a Quebec school were asked to correct the
grammar in Marc Lépine's suicide note.

The student reads it slowly,
careful to avoid the blood
in dark spilled pools.
Everywhere
there are mistakes. She begins
by correcting the spelling,
holding her pen steady
to make small red marks
around the words,
and then she stops, absently
concentrating on a period,
the hole at the end of a sentence, incomplete
nightmare:
for a moment she imagines blood
on pillow and sheets,
blankets, walls, ceiling,
even on her hands. She tries to read it
again, but in this letter
death is a space
between words: the memory of bodies,
lying – as if flung – on the floor
in awkward
syntax.

CHOPPING WOOD

Two miles from home, a man misses
a stroke. The axe
is deep in his leg, the blood too
red, too rich; any vivid colour
has no business in the woods
at a time of year when breath plumes
the air, and snow makes a querulous
sound underfoot. He takes

off his coat quickly,
tears his shirt into strips, hands
trembling. The trick is not
to faint, not to
fall, because if he does no one

will know. He pulls the strip tight,
screaming, yanks the axe
from his flesh. There is a commotion
of birds between one black tree
and another. He staunches the wound,

freezes it, but soon the blood warms
again, leaves an erratic
crimson
trail. He is dying,
or trying not to. What keeps
the body moving towards
rectangles of light? Something hauls him

along, holds him upright: a lace collar
on his wife's dress, the sheen of her hair,
yearning to lie on the downy snow, pillow
of the end, a short sleep. He freezes
the wound again, drags his leg: one step
hell, one step home.

The world turned blue
with storm, trickery
in every leaf. Wind shook us
loose: a sudden
rain was beating at the distant,
terraced slopes
near Siena. The trace of something

parting air. Centuries
of magic. We were artists:
we could see
everything from that hill, going back
hundreds of years, what holds us
back, stripping us
bare, what dresses us in light.
                                   Thunder in our bodies,
fire in our hair.

SALAMANDER

If new legs are grafted
where the old ones were,

the salamander (glistening,
with tiny yellow spots) will grow

new ones anyway. And if
the legs are transplanted

incorrectly, like boots
on the wrong feet, two new legs

will flower below each false
appendage, as if to point out

the error. Perhaps we have the same
capacity when something is misplaced —

like love — and then recovered, even
if we get it wrong, and your

heart flowers on the tip of my
finger, while I respond with several

smaller buds, nested
up and down your spine, all just about

to open when I put my hand there.
You see: such profusion

isn't so improbable. It's only
when the salamander

withholds a trick, doesn't move,
or blink, or sprout another limb

(delicate as the feathered wing
on Hermes' heel) that we remember

the miraculous.

OCTOPUS

Once she saw a man with an octopus
which he beat
      on the concrete stairs
            leading down to the beach.
As she read a book
on a small balcony, she could hear the continuous
thwack, thwack, thwack, thwack
of flesh struck against something solid
to make it tender.
She flipped the book shut, went for a walk
and when she came back
the man was still there, smoking,
but never missing a beat. *Thwack, thwack,*
thwack, thwack. She could hear it
persisting (even when she went inside
and closed the windows in the hotel room)
      monotonously loud
           as something remembered:
one body slapping against another
in the tedium of desire. She opened the book
to read, distracted
by the octopus, dying and dying
in its own noise.

Shave my head,
she told her son. Hair was falling
out in clumps anyway,
and she had no use for it. He didn't
want to do it; think of the care
needed to raze that scalp

egg-smooth. Her husband
came to help and the two of them
worked slowly. She could see
their reflections in the dark
window, felt the little blades
of despair. What if none of this

did any good and she was
pared down
a little at a time? The moon was rising
above the garden, not quite full,
golden and slightly lopsided: a head
like hers. Anything can invade

luminous places. The moon
had marks to show for it.

In that slow, lapping month
I drew the waves around me like a blanket
and moved with the weird, translucent
creatures: the hanging jellyfish,
the fins flashing past,
a crab sidewising the nether sands.
In this brine and spill
I let you go.

Now I lie floating on the sea's hammock
slung at the four corners of sky,
and you open your first eyes
gazing blue and blind
as I trace an ear,
holding your head in my cupped hands.
We lie newly born
tipping from one side to the other,
between water and air.

Sleep with me.
The waves undulate with our breathing,
taking us with the tide
as we roll over and under the sliding dark
doused and dunked like sea otters
clutching a simple meat.
So you grasp and suck,
swallowing the thousand stars
the gulp of moon and the whole sweet sky.

LUNA MOTH

The luna moth was on the outside of the screen, blown
in from the sea. Its lustrous wings were bigger than
my fist – both fists – and white as orchid petals, recalling
something we'd said once about moths. I hadn't imagined
one like this: so large, so pale. Beyond the moth,

I could see the place where the tide went in and out,
and Basket Island, and further off, the spit of land
where people dig for clams. The water was silky
blue moving from tidal pool to ocean, like a tipped
basin. Of course, I thought of your hands,

which had nothing to do with it. I returned to the moth,
examining each gauzy curve, the greenish body
and great wings – a Chinese concubine's earlobes –
clinging to the mesh of wire. Desire is always
dressing itself in something beautiful. Not that glamour

was going to save the moth. It was fighting to survive
or be snapped up by the wind, ending up a bit of taffeta,
a shred of veil or ball gown left over from a party
the night before. I hoped it would live. Maybe
it could dry in the sun, detach itself loosely

from the screen and find its way to you, revealing
what I intended all along. Not the brown moth,
or the yellow, but this one, only this. After a few minutes
the moth subsided, leaving the scrap of its body clinging
to the door. It would never have found you, anyway.

One way or another we end up as fools, like Gilgamesh
poling across the sea of death. Finally, he reaches the other side,

after drifting for days (since the pole rotted in the poisonous
water). Someone wise is waiting on that far shore, but the voyager

has spent himself in grief, that monotony, which is really
only mourning for ourselves. So the quest is reduced to something

simple: who can take pain from us, even briefly, so we don't have to look
into those rooms in the mind, where old lovers are always present

and absent at the same time? Gilgamesh loved Enkidu, not just
as a friend, but also with the piercing of desire that drives

a needle in the flesh and threads it through. Like the flip side
of ourselves, Enkidu is that self we all imagine, hidden

in the forest, by the quiet pool. There are tapestries
revealing such secrets: the eye of the unicorn is full of light

and darkness, but how contentedly the animal lies. Remember
the lover's hand upon the neck, the words that rub here and there

like fingers, caressing. With the slightest touch comes the worry
that something might change, and loneliness will catch on it

and unravel the pattern. And so Enkidu dies, and Gilgamesh, stunned,
tries to revive him. This is where we come into it, with our disbelief,

our letters and photographs laid out on the table, which curl
and yellow in the sun, while the furniture stands implacable as a jury

predicting our demise. Though the wise man takes pity on Gilgamesh
and shows him where to look for the flower of life, it won't

do any good. Who can raise Enkidu from the dead? Still, it's beautiful:
each petal stung scarlet, the way blood looks on a fingertip. And here,

of course, it's lost in the pause of relief, when we spread out on the beach,
feel the sun again, close our eyes, and allow the grip to loosen. Waking,

we find the flower has been stolen; the snake's track is a thin wiggle
of calligraphy on sand. Gone. This is when it sinks in, when we get up

and walk back into our lives, knowing the same thing will happen again.
We learn the lesson the snake teaches: to shed our skins a thousand times

in any given day.

FEEDING THE ANCHORESS

for Julian of Norwich

The light flickers in the white grass,
in the hoarfrost. It is early
and the garden, if there was one,
is covered over and glazed with cold.
She settles herself in the small room
they have made for her beside the cathedral,
listening as they place one stone
above another,
and the *trick, trick* of the trowel
scraping and smoothing the mortar until she is walled in,
enclosed, eyes shut,
fingering the rosary.

She recalls the greens of the garden, bright folds
shaken out in the breeze, irises uncurling in purple,
yellow, tangled with the brazen roses.
Someone brings her food. She turns
away from it, gropes
toward God like a blind mole
feeding on darkness.

MYTH

There were other people moving in that room,
but she was watching the illuminated lenses

of his glasses as he talked about a Russian love story:
a man in love with a woman,

a distant woman, who was, of course, beautiful
and who only fell in love with the man

after a long time, although that wasn't the end of it
(she didn't trust anything so simple

but listened, curious about his glasses,
like mirrors, in which she saw things)

because neither the man nor the woman knew
the depth of the other's love

except that it was a door
opening to another door, until she couldn't think about it

anymore and looked away in the direction
of Orion and the Pleiades through the dark

glass of the window where the stars were obscured
by reflections of people dancing

so that it was impossible
to find what she was looking for. Anyway, it was clear

that constellations weren't really connected
like dot-to-dot figures

except in myths.

MEANWHILE, IN ITHACA

"It may be that Ulysses never left home . . ." – Alberto Manguel

If Ulysses stayed home
instead of going off,
there would have been no maidens
flinging their hair over their shoulders
on a fabulous island, no Circe, no Cyclops,
no sirens calling over the sound of rushing
water. Where do any of us wander
but in the mind, skirting the magical
whirlpools, following a whiff of something,
like a dog? It's the dedication to finding
a bit of sausage, a heel of bread;
fascination with the scent
makes us keen

with wanting. One morning, on a bus,
I saw the whitened face of a mountain
turned rosy. The bus turned a corner
and the mountain was lipped
in brightness – as if it contained secrets
like a tiny door high up, opening on a spring –
when we drew up at the terminal.
The woman next to me may have seen it;

we were speaking of things longed for
and not obtained, or
obtained along with some slight

cost, which no doubt Ulysses tried
to avoid by dreaming of lush places
and leaving his wife to her various men. Whether
they coupled or not was irrelevant. Their desires
unnerved him,

not much different from his own,
except that the imagined
is so much safer
without the minor setbacks,
flesh wounds, sweaty clasp
of arms, the tang of adultery smelling
like a certain kind of cheese. The dog
would find it out, if no one else,
so little bits of life

are left undone. Other people make
the journeys to exotic shores, kiss and
cry when it is over, as it always is
sooner or later, even if
the little door in the mountain
remains open for a moment,
and a wooden figure comes out and twirls,
while something within chimes the hour.

JULY 15, 1887

The engineer sees the freight train
far off, on the St. Thomas crossing,
and tries reversing – forehead slick,
belly tight – when the air brakes don't
work. The fireman scrambles up,
pulling the brake on the baggage car,
and now the engineer reads
Michigan Central Railway
painted yellow on the cars
filled with oil,
while evening glazes the plate
glass windows on Talbot Street,
stretches itself over the low fields,
lingers in these seconds, time elongated
into something about to happen,
in the shape of (the train
and its passengers: my great-great-grandmother
holding her youngest son tightly,
tightly) blue shadows racing over the ground,
over the fireman who has jumped
from the train, skinning his knees as he tumbles,
rolling into the ditch and covering
his ears.

The explosion – so loud
it echoes from that century
to this – breaks the plate glass windows,
shudders houses, sweeps fire

through each car of the train. No one
near it has a chance, not even
the man from the livery stables —
trying to douse flames on the roof —
licked golden as a god
against a sky gone black with smoke.
He stands on the shingles, arms outstretched,
poised to fly.

WHITE, MAUVE, YELLOW

"The bowl does not have colour in itself; light generates the colour."
— Johannes Itten

A bedsheet is suspended on the clothesline
in my neighbour's yard. I am surprised by the
rippling white as the sheet lifts
and exposes the greenish-brown grass below.
This square — although slightly more than a square,
less than a rectangle, opening out in the wind
like a body waiting for another body,
a loosening, stretching
length of singing white on that single
float of wind, appearing whiter because of the mauve
shadow underneath — changes immediately

when the wind slackens. Hanging
like a stranded piece of wing, it is the colour of
something caught, animal or bird
or even the skin at the wrist and the slightly creamy
white of the inner arm, paler than any other part
of the body and more secretive. The sheet snaps briefly,
flips over the clothesline and slaps the air again.

Now it is still, a painful white,
an almost perfect shape,
except for the curling hem and the undulating
pink stripes along the top and bottom. The shadow
on the grass should be taken into account too,

because of its darkness
in contrast, and its shape, which is long
and distinct as a memory, except for one
scrolled edge. My neighbour appears, pulling the line
which makes a sound like a cat crying
as she takes the five pegs out of the sheet,
bundling it in her arms, so that it seems
yellow, heaped up like that, and I imagine her
putting it on a queen-sized bed,
briskly tucking it in, so that it is entirely
flat and smooth.

FLYING EAST

All day I fly east, the wide
floor of prairie below

and cloud, in feathers, sometimes
obscuring it. I feel your hands

where they have never been:
soft against the open land

with its small, frozen lakes, stroking
the brushy pines in northern Quebec,

white roads curving into
nowhere. The plane's wing is tipped

with scarlet, even as the sky
wanes, fading to evening, to blue

and deeper blue as we descend
into Montreal. Cup your hands, draw

up that darkness, full of air
and filigree, outlining the river's absence.

The length of the continent's body
is laid out between us. Lean over, gaze at it.

Recall all the things we didn't say:
those insistent clusters of

lights between parks,
plains, miles of wide spaces

where no one lives.

TWO PHOTOGRAPHS

One of these photographs
shows her standing by a wall:
self-portrait of young woman
who will not show her face.
She holds jagged paper
against her skin
so that only belly, arm, and feet
are visible as she teaches herself
to dissolve
in the elusive, butterfly light.

The other photograph,
taken just before she killed herself,
reveals a figure who is barely there.
Light blown in with the curtains
makes shapes of hair and eyes,
skirt and shoe,
disturbing the tangible
woman standing in a room.
She is only an illusion, after all:
a time-elapsed trick of light
at a certain speed
that makes a bitter image here.

ARCHEOLOGY

Turning itself slowly for the photo op, the visible
world (scarved in cloud, blue and glamorous)

is pictured by satellites four hundred miles
away, with probing cameras that offer proof

of what it's like fifteen feet below the desert,
biting the skin of sand like a needle, or puncturing

a South American rainforest, tangled with green
and sometimes golden light, cluttered with living

things, penetrating all the way to earth. Already,
there are major breakthroughs: a Mayan site,

unplundered, where no one ever considered it,
and a promising target at the head of the Persian Gulf,

which could be the Garden of Eden. Things can be dug up
underwater, and disturbances kept to a minimum.

If there's an Atlantis somewhere, the images (digital
or infrared) will capture it. There's no mystery

to any of this. Think of a city down there, complete
with towers and domes, a glint here and there of fish

swimming through open windows, or a rooftop garden,
where the seaweed floats slowly back and forth

with the currents. It's only the beginning: what lies
beneath the body's thin surfaces, what

ancient cities of pain,
what gardens of delight?

SMALL

We are sliding on the ice; he says we can't
stop, headlights coming closer until death
is a little scarf pulled
through the ears by magic
the brakes catch on something
and the truck whistles
past. Our small

lives given back to us
for the moment
as we imagine wreckage,
parts of the car in the snowy
ditch, limbs askew, things
scattered everywhere: what
might have been.

Think of anything but this,
maybe an insect
turned upside down on a table,
tiny legs bicycling
against air, until something rights it,
lets it go
wherever it wants: into the garden
or back in the glass jar.

Usual Devices

Aphrodite > Hera and Athena.

Paris is only a boy,
choosing between them. What he really wants

is the apple shining in his hand, but they won't let him
keep it. Anyway, it's all based on first impressions.

Hera has power and Athena's got brains. But who sees
these things? Aphrodite has perfect legs,

gilded hair, and blue eyes that open and shut
just like a mortal. He considers, marks each one —

Hera	Aphrodite	Athena
smiled	is all warm smiles	will smile
tricked	and small tricks,	will trick
brought	bringing her little myths	will bring
gave	of love, she gives kisses	will give
desired	like petals, desiring	will desire
took	him, taking whatever	will take
turned	is needed to turn the tables	will turn
decided	and decide the outcome	will decide

— and declares Aphrodite the winner. She laughs,
disappears. The other two pause, gazing at him.

It begins with an apple: heaven's usual device.

,

The servant girl, in a hurry to break the news, gasps
as she races along the path, nearly falling on a tree root:

The queen has gone, sir.

Later, she lies in Menelaus's bed (after he talks, weeps,
lays his head in a willing lap) curled small as a comma

against his back, a hook that catches on something recalled:
the flicker of Helen's skirt seen from a window, at night,

a man's hand, dark against white cloth, on her hip.

∿

Situated in the pause between one thing
and the next. The particulars of absence:

Gone, gone, gone, gone. Menelaus wakes, bitterly
gazing at a girl who is not Helen. No other woman

could be Helen, with her golden sheen, loose hair,
limbs like water. How could she take a lover,

leave? She belonged to him, paid in full (oxen and horses,
not to mention slaves) to her father. He'd been the one

to win her. Gone, gone, gone, gone, gone, gone, gone.
Comma's sharp point sinks into the place between words,

deep in that flesh; nothing moves forward without pain.

!
.

The Greeks have come. The Trojan queen watches
the rumour become a line of ships, lowering

their sails. It begins: measured in years, each
minute marked in blood. Hekuba sees it all before

it happens. She's brought up her children to honour
their family: so they will die, wrapped in shrouds,

one beside the other, all for glory, which is nothing
but a dead hand passed through a living body.

Who'll remember any one of them? They'll end up
the same, eventually, stretched out on a beach,

hacked and torn, wounds marking their chests in red:

!!

The rowers ship their oars, jump into the water
and bring the boats to land. Hekuba closes the shutters,

stands with her back against them. She knows the way it goes:
war is that trick we practise on each other to see

who can last longest without taking a breath.

Daily Tally

Greeks

Dead:	53
Wounded:	12
Missing:	4
Total:	69

Trojans

Dead:	64
Wounded:	26
Missing:	2
Total:	92

Walk among the dead, count the young bodies
piled on the ground. Stinking.

Who has the heart for it? This is one day's work.
Tomorrow, there'll be more,

so many that it's hard to tell one body from
another. Here are parts of what they were:

arms, legs, a dirty foot, someone's helmet, a spear.

Arrange them carefully, hands at their sides,
military fashion. Burn the Greeks together,

according to the rites, watch the smoke rise
– mingling with that of the Trojan dead –

and drift in the air.

=

How much is a woman equal to? Take Briseis,
given to Akhilles as booty: is she worth four oxen?
Six? Her father's allied to the Trojans, which might reduce

her value. But the thighs are fleshy, breasts soft, skin
spread like a banquet. When Agamemnon sees her bending
over the laundry, he waits until she rises, arms slick

and wet, with a stain of water on her clothes. Oh! Yes,
he got the short end of the stick with the priest's daughter
who'll have to be sent home. He'll have this girl instead.

∾

Briseis, taken from the hut, looks back at Akhilles sitting
on the sand. She wavers in his vision, like something
turned to air or mist. She could disappear now,

from the tale and the hero's view. But she continues, braiding
her hair with tears; the king will return her (briefly)
just before Akhilles goes to battle, dies. A woman is equal to

this,
the weight of her grief.

;

Like a warrior who gives a backward
glance, hesitating just long enough to be caught by an arrow,

at the gate between one part of the sentence and the other.
This is the place where Akhilles falters, looking up at Paris,

who stands on the ramparts watching him die. The words that follow
are the faint, papery sounds of a dying man. Semicolon

has an open mouth and something sharp driven in its heel.
The hero dies. Greeks and Trojans skirmish over the body;

something is lost in the dust. Down by the ships, the warriors
begin to think it's futile. They'd better think of something

quickly, to get them out of this mess: a public-relations gimmick,
some sort of trick. It's left to Odysseus to think of a hollow horse

and a plan to save Helen, that bright conjunction between rival
nations. What replaces her when she departs but a wound,

a lick of flame?

♦
♦

Two dots: the beginning and end
of the Trojan wars.
But what goes in between?

Helen.

She sits at her loom thinking
how Paris talked her into it;
how she talked herself into it. Lust

is a snake bite: twin holes
in a wrist. But her wrists
are pale and smooth,

marked only by blue paths
of divergent veins. Colon is two
people. Together,

apart. It offers explanation:
the real cause of any war is one person
spoiling for a fight, fists clenched.

She pushes a thread into place with her weaving comb
to the sound of men in battle.
Warp. Weft. Death's pattern.

≈

Helen considers the weaving she has to do:

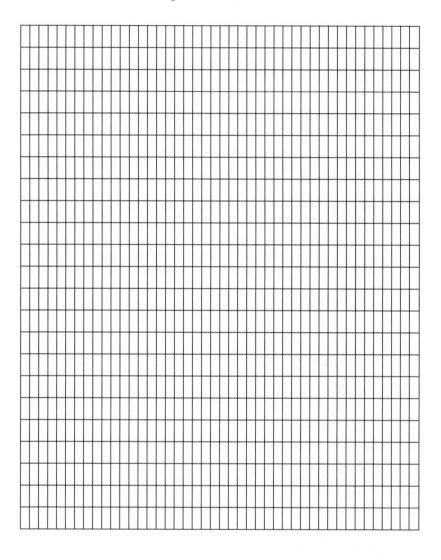

~

At night, Helen thinks of her child, and dreams
of slipping away unnoticed. But there's a rift
in the sentence: two cities separated by water.

When she wakes in the morning, she dresses
and goes out on the ramparts with Priam.
Aphrodite comes close,

takes her by the hand, whispers:

> Where would you go?

> You have no home to go to.

> Do your part.

Colon is one beautiful woman standing by another,
telling her she can't compare.

Who trusts Odysseus? Perhaps he dressed as a beggar,
and went to the gates of Troy, where they beat him,
mocking. Where Helen finds him,

not knowing who he is. In her house, she cleans
each wound delicately. Her fingers are seeds
planted in his skin, and where she touches,

he flourishes, as if in need
of water. What is hidden in parentheses but a glance,
that sharp arc of longing? She hesitates.

Surely it's the body of a king she tends. Catching
her wrist, he holds it until she meets his eyes.
Two people leaning forward,

whispering. (It's Odysseus.) She tells him
things a spy would want to know, then realizes
what she's done. (He won't tell.) Leaving,

he raises a finger to his lips. Away from her
he is a garden
remembering her hands

fingering his deepest places. He yearns
to explain how she opened his body,
bone by bone, then locked it shut again.

?

Priam contemplates the horse.

What?

He gazes at it, then turns and walks the beach,
followed by his men. He stoops
now and then to pick up a few encrusted shells,

which he arranges on the palm of his hand,
grouping them, like a good host,
in small familiar clusters. Then he tosses

the handful away. The tide can take
them. After years of war, he is without
pity, only habit and method: his kingdom

is sand.

It is raining lightly again; the beach
slick with water, irresolute
streams that dissolve

in the licking sea. He looks out,
where there is nothing: no boat, no sail.
But the sea outwits the beach each time.

What is left?

The waves repeat their funerals, tirelessly
returning for more. They heap themselves
– shimmering, breaking –

women over dead bodies.

~

Priam returns to the horse.

Why?

The Greeks have fled, taking the shoring timbers
from the boats, pushing them into the water,
loosing the sails to the wind. Priam watched them go,

indifferent.

What does war teach
in the end? Its heroes are turned to stone
and set up in public squares: here is another

nobody remembers.

It's done, Priam thinks. No more can come of it.

Why not?

The snake wrapped its coils around Laokoön;
they struggled in the water. Who's to say
where this will stop? It goes on

and on, relentlessly. Even afterwards,
the sea asks
its question in different ways, chant

and chorus: Is this the end,
or this? The king
puts his hands to his head, covers his eyes.
Perhaps he's going mad. He straightens,

gives command: Wheel it in.

◆

The end of a long sentence about war.

The odd fire still burns in the city. The Greeks look up
from the beach, where they have divided the spoils:

several women over there, some over here. Victory is
an anticlimax, hardly noticed in the midst of the work

that needs to be done. They leave as mist rises,
exposing what remains: a war that hasn't ended.

It's the hole we fall into again and again.
We fumble in the trenches, gathering our medals

and letters. Then it's time. Our finest hour is the one
no one sees. There's a pause in the march of words,

all moving in the same direction. A breath, a gasp.
Until the sentence takes it up again, trumpeting a theme

of glory, grown stale with time. But from a Greek ship, far
out on the water, comes a woman's keening, high and wild.

Reliquary

RELIQUARY

"The red soil of heaven is in the grave." – Traditional (from the Yoruba)

Here is a bone resembling a word. And ribs, some still intact, holding
something that isn't there. These fragments were a person. (Get up and
sing. Tell all.) Someone swung a machete and severed head from spine.
(Sing. Get up. Twirl once, lie down.) Then the red earth folded up the
body and let it seep down, bit by bit. Over here: a tooth. Not gold. Who
can hear the sound a ghost makes, biting on air?

~

Let us translate as whispers, as pauses. A little dust on the table. On the
floor.

~

This was a woman. Remember the mermaid turned to foam? She floats
on red ground, part of her already lost. Twisted by the cloth. Her face is
covered, though no face is left. There were small flowers on the cloth,
once. She has no legs. No hands. (Sing. Sing.) No feet. Still, the skull
remains, with its cloth. Stitch the cloth to the earth. It keeps down the
screams after dark.

~

Arms raised gracefully, the way we raised our arms as children, making
feathery wings. Angels in snow. These bones are imprints.

~

Here are bones ending in high-heeled shoes that used to be red. The soles are peeling away, but the bones of the feet are still fitted to them. From the knees up, the skeleton is covered with a cloth. Like the body next to it, and the one over there. There are hundreds like this. Each is a wing, a part of a wing, or a travesty of a wing.

~

Where do we dare to look?

~

Imagine fossils. The beauty of a fragile thing, like a fern, for instance, pressed into rock. Imagine a child pressing against its mother, if the child and the mother are long dead.

~

The few ribs are whitened. They curve like fingers when the palm is up, resting on something solid. They ask. They beg.

~

The skulls are kept together, eggs in a basket. Each one is slightly different: white, rust-coloured, brown, discoloured, mottled, cracked. A man reaches down and picks one that is riddled with holes. He holds it carefully, with both hands.

~

A skull is a verb that can't be conjugated. Not *amo*, not *amas*, not *amat*.

~

Some rocks in the garden at home could be skulls. One is bald and rounded, sunk in the dirt. Dig it out, clean it, put it in a place where it catches the light. On top of the piano, perhaps, next to the orange begonias.

~

All of us luminous objects. Like rocks in the garden.

~

Light is an axe through the top of our heads. It splits us open, and for one moment we see.

~

Then silence. A field of it.

~

The little door swings shut in the air. Here is a bone, a padlock.

Altarpiece

ALTARPIECE

I

The sprinkler makes its perfect arc, forward and back:
a fan, beaded with tiny gems. Further along,
workmen are tearing up asphalt to plant blue
water mains and the early-morning light slants
over a lawn, its fine blades unhampered by weeds.
Only at the farthest margin a burnt fringe shows: no rain.
None for weeks. The sprinkler's fragile
threads fall to earth, daintily. A woman
in a terry-cloth robe picks at her potted geraniums,
a green van pulls out of a driveway, tinted windows rolling
up, sealing the driver inside. Here is the golf course:
the man-made hills sliding open to a view of steel factories
across the bay. Already the sky is clouded, baroque,
with something pinkish-yellow and stinking.
This grass is clipped close as a shaved face: touch it –
you might be amazed it's real. Someone stops
to cross the road, looking from one side to the other.
Her legs are golden, and the white tassels of her golf shoes swing
and bobble as she strides. We are at the end of a century.
It slopes away from us, the green sliced by knives of light
as far as the polluted lake.

II

Imagine this as a painting by a German artist
in the sixteenth century: a man in a golf cart,
the flesh of his gut covered by a red jersey, and a girl
– hair shimmering – using a leaf blower in the parking lot.
No vaguely green Christ dies on a cross with fingers splayed,
no one mourns. This is not quite the tail end of the remembered –
last kiss, last breath, when everything freezes for a moment
in fright: the squirrel hesitating before it scampers
to the soft verge, luxuriant depths of green at the edge
of the golf course, where crickets hum with pleasure. But
it's also not the beginning, or the various wars between:
a million scratches on a surface. This has to do with where we are
now, light floating lazily down, further
and further, through the tracery of willow leaves.

III

A child is whacked on the side of the head by another
with a hockey stick yelling "motherfucker." The child sags,
head bloody. It didn't happen here, where morning has a sweet
stupidity about it. Here, green acorns fall to the pavement – *snak,*
snak – and a single cardinal dips from a bough like a hand
pulling a red thread. The somnolent windows of the houses
heavy-lidded with blinds. *Snak.* A fox elegantly
crosses the road, as a man in a car brakes, realizing he's never
seen a fox in his life. And a boy picks up his bike –
awkwardly, since he's carrying a hockey stick – and goes home,
leaving the other sprawled, blood seeping into the grass, red
into green. The fox insinuates itself through a hole in a hedge,
strolling over the lawn, tail plumed like a Prussian
general's feather. A border of impatiens locks the animal
into the green square. Whatever happened will happen again.

IV

A boy and his sister braid footprints through light snow
along the Tiergartenstrasse when they see the headlines:
Hitler has been proclaimed chancellor
as predicted. Still, people go about their business,
like Saint Sebastian calmly praying in Grünewald's altarpiece,
neck pierced by an arrow just above the clavicle. Where
does the century lead us? Not to the path of salvation,
or the fork in the woods where the horse balks. It brings us
here, to the green lawn.

V

Tock. The golfer waits for a ball to land in the right
place, which it never does. A fox executes
a jump into someone's snapdragons. And a painted lamb
at the feet of Grünewald's dying Christ tilts its head
to let blood stream into the golden chalice. (O tender
gift.) Now the golf ball is carefully putted; it circles around
and drops like a penny in a can. A child returns
home, lets his bicycle crash, opens the broken screen door
with his hockey stick. A black squirrel scoops an acorn
and races across a lawn newly sprayed with pesticides.
One thing more: two girls discover an unconscious child,
leaning over him without knowing what to do.

VI

And above this, brilliant spume in the darkness,
the spit of gods. Things repeat themselves in glorious
pattern – the spiral of the galaxy, the hurricane, water
going down the drain – endlessly. Even Grünewald's Mary
(bent in sorrow, the shock of her white veil against the black)
makes a shape that recurs. She is translating herself,
each hand a star. We should have seen it coming, that
shift from lament to indifference. But the sprinkler interrupts
– *chukka, chukka, chukka, chukka* – as it uses up another round
of ammunition. And begins again. Christ repeats his agony,
ladies weep, saints commence, once more, the task
of comforting. And we avert our eyes. A woman
in a terry-cloth robe folds the paper, sips a blend of Kenyan
in a blue mug, takes off her glasses to watch a fox
trample the snapdragons and saunter through the roses. Indolence
is the best way out: animals sleep whenever possible.

VII

Nothing imagined – not with the scent of fairy roses
hanging innocent as prom dresses on the air – nothing
concluded. Everything stutters. We are capable only of observation,
like the astronomer with his homemade telescope in the backyard,
set up for every kind of miracle: light crinkling like tin foil,
planets dissolving, the dim, the distant, the chalky smudge
of a far-off world brought close. A dark minefield. The sky –
the background of the altarpiece – might be negative space,
though we know it's a distraction from the ugliness
of Christ's dead body. In the blue-black of the painting,
anyone can hear the shriek of one star slamming into another,
a gnashing in the outer cloakroom, or the tinkle – fine as crystal –
of bones in the divine chandelier. It's all easier looking down
on the floating globe, the kingdoms of lawn, the artistic detail
of a woman glancing up through the window to find the fox
vanished. She gets up, slowly, as depressed women do,
and makes a spiral around the kitchen looking for her glasses
(on the table by the folded newspaper). How tiny
she is at this distance. How small her feelings, especially
when she cries over the newspaper story of the boy in a coma,
the murmurs of his body faint as an asteroid coming this way.

VIII

The golf course is draped with curtains
of leaves, attended by funereal shadows. The hush deepens
towards midday – just cicada drill and the odd whirr
of a cart. This is the hour when an angel steps into the painting,
wings brushing knick-knacks from the shelves. Mary turns
away. Dread comes of looking at something squarely,
like the little shawls of skin hanging from trees
after an airplane crashes. Behold
the handmaiden of the Lord. A warbler's trills are ringlets
of ribbon on a cake box. In backyards near the golf course,
swimming pools dazzle and confuse. The angel departs
in a rustle of gown and feathers, leaving Mary to think
things over, her mind a fox moving between the skunk cabbage
and jewelweed. Its paw disturbs a mystical
sleeve of leaf. And a child sighs in his coma.
Time claps us awake, and we arrive disoriented – like the rest
of the refugees – at the border. One country is memory,
and the other blessing, where we forget everything we ever knew.

IX

Surely if we roused ourselves, someone would recall
the proper grammar for this moment? Divine passive voice.
The baby is born in the central panel of the altarpiece,
angels buzz in the honeycomb of heaven. Listen
to the world offering congratulations: the golfer birdies
on the ninth (*tock, tock*), the crane drops a section of blue
water main into the hole, effusive diamonds of applause
issue from the sprinklers. Even in the hospital
the child's sleeping skin is warm: touch his face
gently, running fingers over his closed eyes, wrapped skull.

X

"The cardinals are singing," thinks the woman, hanging
her robe on the bathroom door and taking a good look
at her body in the mirror. Light from the window gilds
her arm, magnifies a thousand fine hairs between wrist
and elbow, caresses the rounded stomach
with its shiny snail tracks, souvenirs of birth. (Note the details –
each exquisite brushstroke – of the painting.) The medication
keeps it all in check. She draws a curtain as she gets into the shower:
what's recalled of beauty now?

XI

The golfer orders a club sandwich, thinking of crisp bacon
and tomatoes, layer on layer. Outside, light floods the golf course
in early afternoon, harshly, so the grass appears drier than it is.
Watering systems everywhere have been turned off
until evening, that blue comfort longed for in the heat of the day.
A woman tries to nap, but the Nazi barks of the crow
invade the room. *Ja, ja*. Invade her brain.
In the painting, Saint Anthony struggles to ward off demons
of temptation. See the beast with its topaz eye, raising a cudgel
to strike. Another with shark teeth, folded lips, nosing closer.
The brazen things are gathering, waiting to pounce.

XII

Far away, a little yolk of radiance appears in the sky,
and something waves, the wing of an angel, or a fluorescent
hand in the windshield of a truck. Have a good day. On the street,
bright orange signs show figures digging, each with its head
popped off like a cannonball. Here the water mains will be laid,
bodies in a pit. And the century spins slower, slower, until the wheel
— *click, click, click* — seems to stop at $10,000, but ends up at
Miss A Turn. The doctor pulls back the curtain at the boy's bed,
makes a note. The woman dozes on her white eiderdown
while the fox turns on a bed of leaves. Now the phantoms rise
from their ditches, out from behind the trees. Look,
it's only me. In the painting, the demons gain the upper hand.
The golfer pays his bill. *Memento mei.* He goes outside, clutching
the rail as blood rushes to his head. Then everything falls into place
again. A silver Jaguar glides around the drive, the cicadas drone,
the gardener coils a hose. Smaller now, and older, all of us.
Someone almost opens his eyes in a still afternoon, hears
a spasm of laughter down the hall. Nearly wakes to pain in his head.

XIII

The boy slips, floats at the surface of dreams,
scenes shot from an airplane winging tipsily
over water. A long, slow roll to the left,
and a long, slow roll to the right. Now up and up
the face of the mountains, past snowy lip, hanging
valley, summit, and — don't look —
vertiginous descent to the moraine, a highway
through the folds of rock. Here's the century
in living colour. Skim over the little insects
(*cirque aux puces*) waging a world war in miniature,
thousands dying at this very moment. A tiny
Russian staggers, waving his arms, before he falls
face-down in snow. Over here, an intimate little group
is being buried alive. Without pausing, drop
and swoop through a Polish city, gritty black and white,
empty except for a diminutive child carrying a chair
on his head through a street of ashes. Everyone else
has fled. Some are hiding: you won't catch them.

XIV

Now the sound goes wobbly: dissolve to a cartoon
Christ – Grünewald's – rising from the dead
among the Roman soldiers. In the middle of the night
He's twinkling like a fiery Tinkerbell. Far off,
a puffery of cloud, expanding orange, red, gold:
the culmination of all that humans could strive to create
in a lifetime. Dive at the sight.
Plunge deep in the Pacific and surface with the wreckage,
the ethereal city shattered in sticks. The century is printed
on our skins, silk kimono patterns cover our arms, our wrists.
Pretty cranes of our destruction. Forget, forget – soft
blooms nod in the fields everywhere – forget all we have done.
The fox uncurls its body, lithe black legs. The woman
sits up and combs her hair. But the injured boy doesn't
wake. Not yet. His mother sits by his bed, waiting,
under a relentless light.

XV

And nothing more than this. A postscript of light
suffuses everything with gold: each leaf haloed,
grass feathered bright. A lone golfer returns
to the clubhouse. In Grünewald's painting,
there's a final lesson: how the saints endure
their torments, always with a view to the hills,
glistening like rock candy. In the divine distance
minutes tick away and vultures tap beaks on a branch.
Park your golf cart under the sign. The end is never
nigh. There's always a second chance, a way back
into the impossible: Dorothy's ruby slippers.
Shut your eyes, count to three. Look, we're home
at the magical hour of dusk, just when we thought
we'd never make it. Here you are, and you,
and you, most beloved of them all.

XVI

It's quiet on the golf course. The lake glimmers
secretively. And the sky is pricked by needle points
of light. Imagine threading it, star by slippery star.
How easy to miss the destination, waves tossing
us deep into ourselves. We end up somewhere
on night's sea, as one century passes into another,
changing shape – head under wing – as easily
as a bird on water. In her bedroom, the woman turns
out the light. She hears wind chimes, perhaps
her own bones jingled by the breeze. The fox rests
head on paws. And a mother soothes her child's forehead
with a cloth. Nightmares are over, and now sleep
folds up these panels, closes them breath by breath.

The epigraph for "Meanwhile, in Ithaca," comes from a phrase in Alberto Manguel's introduction to Frederick Barthelme's story, "Cut Glass," in *The Second Gates of Paradise: The Anthology of Erotic Short Fiction*.

Information about the train wreck in "July 15, 1887" comes from an account in the *Tillsonburg Liberal* on July 17, 1887.

"Two Photographs" was inspired by the photographic work of Francesca Woodman.

The epigraph for "White, Mauve, and Yellow" is from Johannes Itten's *The Art of Colour: The Subjective Experience and Objective Rationale of Colour*, originally published as *Kunst der Farbe*.

The fragment – an epigraph – preceding "Reliquary" comes from a traditional song of the Yoruba, "Incantation to Cause the Rebirth of a Dead Child," found in *Poems of Black Africa*, edited by Wole Soyinka. "Reliquary" depended on an article, "Rwanda's ghosts scream bloody murder," by Claude Adams and Patricia Chew, published in the *Globe and Mail* on April 4, 1998.

Several ideas led to the writing of "Altarpiece." Eric Hobsbawm's *Age of Extremes: The Short Twentieth Century* begins with "The Century: A Bird's Eye View," in which Isaiah Berlin is quoted as saying, "I remember it only as the most terrible century in Western history." Hobsbawm himself points out that the century "appears like a triptych," in which the first, cataclysmic era of war was followed by a time of comparative calm, giving way to the unease of the *fin de siècle*. Hobsbawm's notion of a triptych led to my unearthing a reproduction of Matthias Grünewald's *Isenheim Altarpiece* (1513-15), which also inspired this poem.

In Section IV of "Altarpiece," I drew on a personal story of Hobsbawm's and took some liberties with it, placing the scene on the Tiergartenstrasse. He observes: "For this author the 30 January 1933 is not simply an otherwise arbitrary date when Hitler became Chancellor of Germany, but a winter afternoon in Berlin when a fifteen-year-old and his younger sister were on the way home from their neighbouring schools in Wilmersdorf to Halensee and, somewhere on the way, saw the headline. I can see it still, as in a dream."

ACKNOWLEDGEMENTS

Some of these poems were first published in the following journals: *Arc*, *Pottersfield Portfolio*, *Room of One's Own*, *The Antigonish Review*, *The Fiddlehead*, and *The Malahat Review*. Others were published in the following anthologies: *Vintage 1999* (League of Canadian Poets) and *Words Out There: Women Poets in Atlantic Canada* (Roseway: 1999), edited by Jeanette Lynes.

"Salamander" was a runner-up for the 1998 Ralph Gustafson Poetry Prize, *The Fiddlehead*.

"Meanwhile, in Ithaca" won second prize in the *Arc* Poem of the Year Contest in 1998.

"Usual Devices" received Honourable Mention in the League of Canadian Poets' Annual Chapbook Competition in 1998.

∼

"Two Photographs" is dedicated to the memory of Francesca Woodman, a young and gifted American photographer.

∼

I am grateful for the Nova Scotia Arts Council Creation Grant that allowed me the time to write many of these poems.

Special thanks to Ellen Seligman, who opened the door.

To Don McKay, my editor – whose keen eye and gentle way with words nudged this manuscript into shape – deepest thanks for believing in these poems.

A cheer to all who participated in the Banff Centre for the Arts Writer's Studio of 1997. And to those who offered criticisms regarding some of these poems – Pamela Black, Dale Estey, Sue Goyette, Mary Fallert, Jeanette Lynes, Pam MacLean, Paul Marquis, Joanne Page, Sue Sinclair, Eddy Yanofsky, and Jan Zwicky – I am indebted to you all. An affectionate wave to Heather and Andy Martin, who said it could be done. And a tribute to the memory of Bronwen Wallace, who helped so much at the beginning.

My family has been especially generous in helping me find precious time to write. Loving thanks to Jan and Jack Simpson, and to Paul, David and Sarah.